AUTHOR C. HEIMLICH PH.D.

Super Bee Ryu- Bee

Saves The Day

- The Problem solving Arthropod
- The bee that can see
- A ringer of a stinger
- The danger Ranger
- He Detects and protects

Knowledge is Power !

Super Bee RyuBee

THE PROBLEM SOLVING ARTHROPOD

All the kids just sat and sat.

They couldn't do this or couldn't do that.

Though the day is nearly gone. Do we

Know   the difference between right and wrong?

AUTHOR C.HEIMLICH PH.D.

THE PROBLEM SOLVING ARTHROPOD

My parents told me to stay alert.

This can help me from getting hurt.

Super Bee RyuBee

THE PROBLEM SOLVING ARTHROPOD

My friend Super-bee Ryu bee has helped me and shown me how to make a stand.

He has taught me how to understand.

Now I Know how to Take command.

AUTHOR C.HEIMLICH PH.D.

THE PROBLEM SOLVING ARTHROPOD

Super Bee Ryu Bee is a friend you see.

A friend to all, he shall always bee.

If ever in need you may call on he.

And Super Bee Ryu Bee will answer thee.

Super Bee RyuBee

THE PROBLEM SOLVING ARTHROPOD

Danger can be a thing of the past.

When you learn to run really fast.

AUTHOR C. HEIMLICH PH.D.

THE PROBLEM SOLVING ARTHROPOD

If you want to Stay Safe From harm and not live in a box Don't answer the door when a stranger Knocks.

SOUND the ALARM

Super Bee RyuBee

THE PROBLEM SOLVING ARTHROPOD

When in eminent Danger always remember the
   "Bug Method"

Flea Flea and still-you shall surely Bee

AUTHOR C. HEIMLICH PH.D.

THE PROBLEM SOLVING ANTHROPOD

(Riddle) When is a (flee) really a bee?

It's not ever wrong to run from danger.

Especially when its from a stranger.

So if you decide that you must flea.

Then again tomorrow you shall surely bee.

Super Bee ryu bee says really think about this one

Super Bee RyuBee

**Super Bee Ryu bee says:
"trust your instincts and when in doubt find an adult to help you out
  Bee sure that your safe where ever you go! and bee with some one that you trust and know"**

AUTHOR C. HEIMLICH PH.D.

Another day the Ryu—bee way

No Stranger should EVER tell you what to do

It's a sign of danger and the biggest clue !

No stranger should ever try to touch you in

any way

If this happens kick, run, scream and

Get- a -way !

If a stranger should ever ask anything of you

Don't look, Don't answer, and Don't leave

Slow !!!

Find some one around that you think you may know waste no Time , you must go go go !

Super Bee RyuBee

Bee with a Friend

If I had a Cat
that could do all that

Or even a dog
 that can see in the fog

Or may be a hog
that rolls like a log

Or how a bout a bear
that I CAN TAKE ANY WHERE

Or just a friend that I can trust
for we should not be alone
that's a MUST

AUTHOR C. HEIMLICH PH.D.

Better than that I can have
an E.T.
A black belt E.T.
What better for me
We can both train in KARATE

How safe will we
Now always bee

Super Bee RyuBee

Some of Super Bee's words of Wisdom

"Detection is the key to protection"

Most People utter 20,000 words a day

What have you said today ?

Even a broken Clock, is right twice a day

AUTHOR C. HEIMLICH PH.D.

My mommy and my Daddy have this
Special "Code".
 it is a very secret Word that no body
 else ever knowde
This secret "CODE" word will keep us safe and secure
From a strangers lies or a dangerous lure
Now you too can have this special word but don't tell
any one not even a bird

Super Bee RyuBee

Detect and Protect

Now Super Bee-Ryu Bee wants to Know What do you do to Protect yourself From a Foe

AUTHOR C. HEIMLICH PH.D.

Always use Caution

All us Bee's we
Can SING, SING,
SING
All us bee's can STING, STING,
STING
What would you do
when you see a bee
as he just sung

Stayyyyy !
Awayyyy !
cause ya might
get
STUNG

Super Bee RyuBee

STRANGER DANGER

The Stranger

Now do you see....What we must do To Protect ourselves From you Know Who ?

AUTHOR C. HEIMLICH PH.D.

Golden rule

Hey Kids
Next Time you get home
From school Don't forget the
#1 RULE
Home work FIRST
Get it done
Then all day long you can have fun ,fun, fun

Super Bee RyuBee

For Good Health

Every one
Wins.....

When ever you take
Your
VITA-MINS....

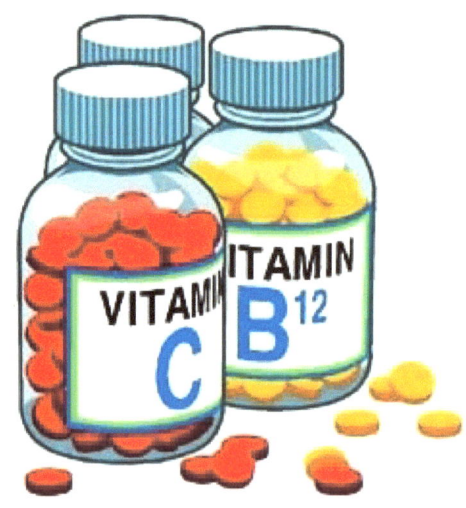

AUTHOR C. HEIMLICH PH.D.

Stay Healthy

So don't ever forget
Take 'em
Every day
So you can Keep
Healthy in every
WAY

Super Bee RyuBee

Sleep is important

Go to Bed early…..
Get lots of Rest…..
When you wakeup…..
You'll feel……..
Your Best !!!

AUTHOR C.HEIMLICH PH.D.

Hold 30 seconds each

Remember when you get up
Out of bed
S>>T>>>R>>>E>>T>>C>>>H
 Out Your body
From toes to Head

Super Bee RyuBee

don't fear anything
___

Think about the things you do !
For the action you take will come back to you.

Make a decision but be very clear, as long as its good you have nothing to Fear

AUTHOR C. HEIMLICH PH.D.

Bee Smart

Remember This,
My little Friends,
Success does not come to you !!!!
you must always go to it !!!!

And don't walk **RUN**

Super Bee RyuBee

My Friend Bumble bee Ben , Ben Franklin that is once Said ,
A smile is a curve that can set a number of things straight.

And did you Know that it takes more muscles to frown than it does to Smile

So smile a while

my little Crocodile

AUTHOR C. HEIMLICH PH.D.

study the Dictionary

The only time "success" comes before "work" is in the "dictionary"

When is the last time you looked in the dictionary

Its True Google it

Super Bee RyuBee

A bully is a Coward

What is a bully

And what should you do to protect your self from you know who

If you ever run into or ever see

The most rude and mean person known as the BULLY

And if they decide to pick on you just walk away with nothing to say but be alert as not to get hurt and if they wont leave you alone speak up and tell them with a strong tone

Stop it now for this isn't right and there is no reason for us to have to fight then get help from any grown up

AUTHOR C.Heimlich Ph.D.

Dreams do come True

Super Bee Ryu Bee would like to say you guys are the greatest in every way so don't ever give up or ever give in dreams can come true but its up to you and only

YOU

*Supper Bee saves the Day with his enlightenment to the children
As they spend their day working out problems and coming up with solutions
As well as many other safety tips*

*Remember kids I'm here to help
Always work Smarter not Harder !*

drprotection@comcast.net

Books By Heimlich

AUTHOR C.HEIMLICH PH.D.

www.ingramcontent.com/pod-product-compliance
Lightning Source LLC
LaVergne TN
LVHW071030070426
835507LV00002B/94